AF228313

NONFICTION
COMPANION
TO
Kimberly Brubaker
Bradley's
The War That Saved My Life

Lisa Kurkov

Rourke
Educational Media

BEFORE, DURING, AND AFTER READING ACTIVITIES

Before Reading: Building Background Knowledge and Academic Vocabulary

Before Reading strategies activate prior knowledge and set a purpose for reading. Before reading a book, it is important to tap into what your child or students already know about the topic. This will help them develop their vocabulary and increase their reading comprehension.

Questions and activities to build background knowledge:
1. Look at the cover of the book. What will this book be about?
2. What do you already know about the topic?
3. Let's study the Table of Contents. What will you learn about in the book's chapters?
4. What would you like to learn about this topic? Do you think you might learn about it from this book? Why or why not?

Building Academic Vocabulary
Building academic vocabulary is critical to understanding subject content.
Assist your child or students to gain meaning of the following vocabulary words.

Content Area Vocabulary
Read the list. What do these words mean?

- *air raids*
- *apprenticeship*
- *canter*
- *chilblains*
- *dictator*
- *evacuees*
- *jodhpurs*
- *Luftwaffe*
- *malnutrition*
- *propaganda*
- *rationing*
- *Victory Garden*

During Reading: Writing Component

During Reading strategies help to make connections, monitor understanding, generate questions, and stay focused.
1. While reading, write in your reading journal any questions you have or anything you do understand.
2. After completing each chapter, write a summary of the chapter in your reading journal.
3. While reading, make connections with the text and write them in your reading journal.
   a) Text to Self – What does this remind me of in my life? What were my feelings when I read this?
   b) Text to Text – What does this remind me of in another book I've read? How is this different from other books I've read?
   c) Text to World – What does this remind me of in the real world? Have I heard about this before? (news, current events, school, etc.)

After Reading: Comprehension and Extension Activity

After Reading strategies provide an opportunity to summarize, question, reflect, discuss, and respond to text. After reading the book, work on the following questions with your child or students to check their level of reading comprehension and content mastery.
1. What did most children do during WWII? (Summarize)
2. Why did they need to do that? (Infer)
3. Why kinds of things do you think the children brought with them? (Asking Questions)
4. Where do you think you would go if you had to move suddenly? (Text-to-Self Connection)

Extension Activity
With a partner, look up some of the interviews mentioned in this book. List two things that were fun about leaving the cities and two things that were difficult.

TABLE OF CONTENTS

Kimberly Brubaker Bradley is an award-winning young people's author. She enjoys writing historical fiction, particularly the stories of individuals. Bradley lives on a farm and raises horses, so the appearance of horses in the novel is no surprise.

In the novel, Bradley tells the story of Ada, a girl growing up in London during World War II. Ada was born with a clubfoot. When she has the chance to escape her difficult home life and evacuate to the countryside, Ada jumps on it. Susan Smith is hesitant, but she takes in Ada and her brother, Jamie. Ada's life changes as she forges a relationship with Susan, a pony named Butter, and a world she never knew existed. Bradley's heartwarming story of Ada's journey continues in *The War I Finally Won*.

Write On!

Although Bradley has now written 17 books, she almost didn't become a writer! She was on track to become a doctor, but literature stole her heart—which is very lucky for her readers.

If you'd like to watch a short video of Bradley discussing The War That Saved My Life, *search the author's name and the book title on* YouTube *for an interview by Penguin Middle School.*

The town that Ada and Jamie are sent to as **evacuees** is a nameless, fictional place. But it is based on the county of Kent in southeast England, about an hour away from London by train.

Bradley didn't choose a real town because a fictional location gave her more freedom in her storytelling. However, just as the residents of Susan's town do in the novel, the people of Kent played an important role in helping the soldiers who were rescued from Dunkirk.

The Battle of Britain was also fought directly over Kent in the summer of 1940. Germany planned to invade southern England in the fall, and the bombings of airfields and harbors were the groundwork for the attack. Luckily, Germany postponed the invasion, which never ended up happening.

Operation Fortitude

A LONDON CHILDHOOD

From the Novel

Before Ada moves to the countryside, she occupies herself by watching the bustle of life on London's crowded streets below her window.

Despite the war, children in London still made time for play. Popular toys and games often had a wartime theme. Playing cards were also popular because they were inexpensive and easy to bring into a bomb shelter to help pass the time.

Bomb sites were an exciting, although dangerous, place to play. There, children could search the rubble for small, interesting treasures. When American soldiers arrived in Britain, anything related to American culture became popular—particularly candy and chewing gum.

Scout's Honor

*Girl Guides and Boy Scouts helped the war effort in a variety of ways. Girls were encouraged to plant vegetable gardens and practice sewing and mending skills. Older boys could have **apprenticeships** and learn trades, such as the repair and maintenance of aircraft. And both groups relayed messages for the Civil Defence Services, a volunteer organization, during the war.*

POVERTY AND POOR HEALTH

Ada's clubfoot has a significant impact on her life. Her mother blames it for the abuse and neglect Ada suffers, and it keeps her from running and playing like other children. Until she visits a doctor with Susan, Ada has no idea that her condition is treatable.

Clubfoot is a condition present at birth caused by the abnormal development of a foot or both feet. In Ada's case, one foot is turned so that the bottom is facing up. Though her mother is cruel to her and mocks Ada for her foot, the condition is relatively common, with one in 1,000 babies having clubfoot. Treatment is fairly simple, and it won't return once it is fixed.

But without treatment, the condition worsens as the child grows. And not all countries have access to the procedure. Around 80% of clubfoot cases occur in countries or populations where prejudice or poverty hinders the ability to get treatment. Some children today still face the same difficulties that Ada does.

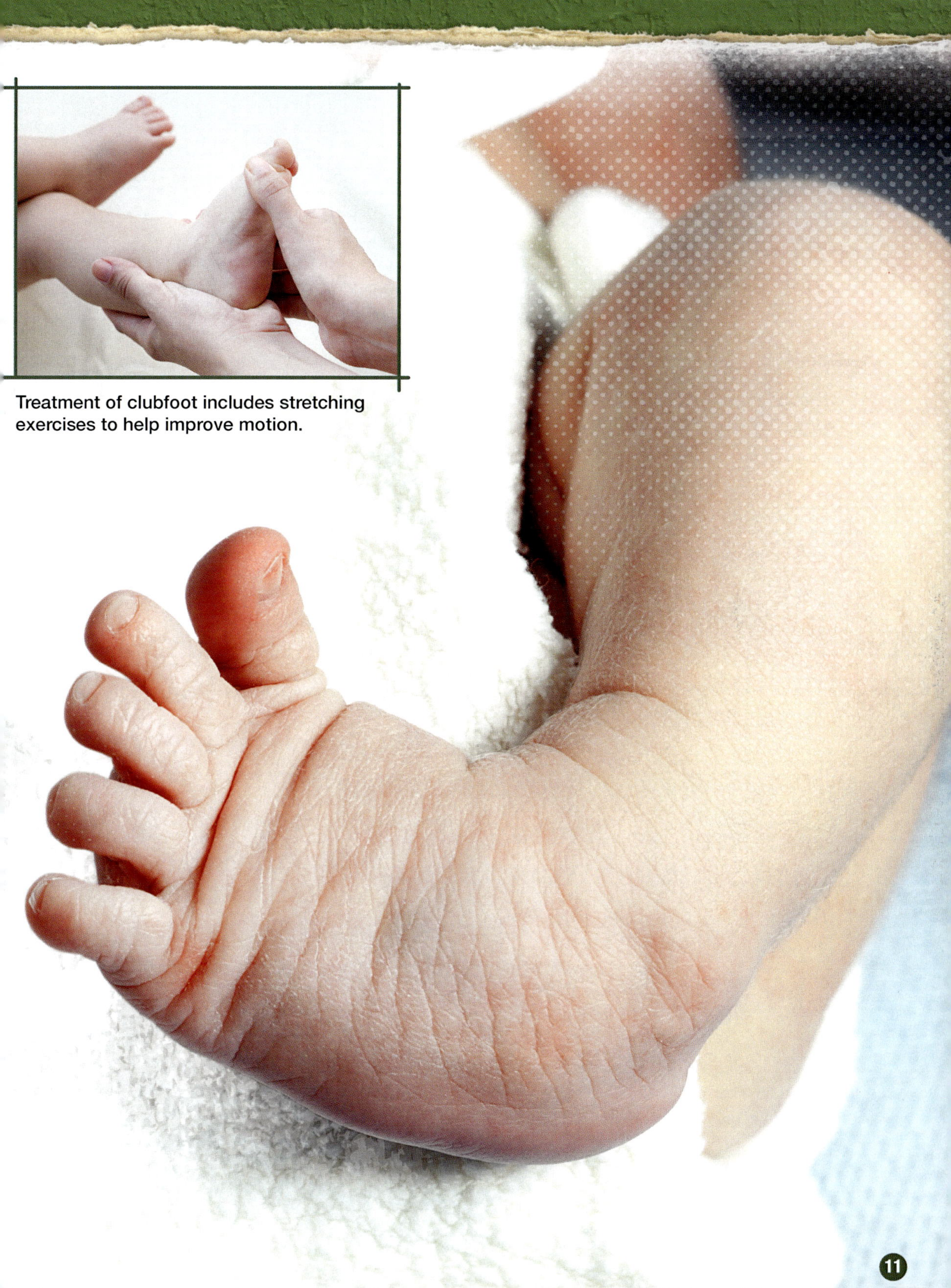

Treatment of clubfoot includes stretching exercises to help improve motion.

Poor children in wartime London were at risk for illness. Impetigo, a contagious skin infection, was common. People lived in close quarters, and indoor plumbing was rare in impoverished areas. This made it easy for illness to spread. Rickets, another common condition, resulted from **malnutrition**, particularly a lack of vitamin D and calcium. Rickets causes bones to become soft and weak and can even cause skeletal deformities.

Chilblains were also linked to poverty. When skin is exposed to very cold air, chilblains can occur. The red, itchy patches blistered and swelled on children who had few warm clothes and often lived in poorly heated homes.

TO THE COUNTRY

From the Novel

Ada and Jamie evacuate to the countryside along with hundreds of other London schoolchildren. They travel by train, unsure of what to expect when they arrive at their destination.

As the war grew closer, the British government needed a plan to keep people safe. The Government Evacuation Scheme focused on getting schoolchildren, mothers with infants, and the elderly to safer locations. Two days before the war officially began, Operation Pied Piper went into effect, and the evacuation of children to the countryside began. Over 600,000 unaccompanied children evacuated from England in the first three days.

Though the program was voluntary, most parents thought it was the best option. Schools regularly held evacuation drills to prepare students. Students brought bags with their necessities to school each day and carried them home in the evenings.

False Alarm

This early period is sometimes called the Phoney War. The lack of bombs made many parents feel safe. Some, like Ada's friend Stephen White's mother, went to retrieve their children. However, the invasion of France and the start of **air raids** *on Britain led to another evacuation. This time, children even went overseas to North America, Australia, New Zealand, and South Africa.*

When the evacuees arrived, they had no idea what they'd find. Some host families chose girls, thinking they would help with the housework. Other families preferred older boys who could work on a farm. In addition to being away from their families, the evacuees often had to get used to changes in housing, food, dialect, and religion.

Sometimes the change was a welcome one. Some children remember being outfitted in new clothing by their host family. Others remember new books, learning about farm chores, or seeing the ocean for the first time.

A Day in the Life

Do an online search for BBC and Interviews with Evacuated Children. You'll be able to see photographs of evacuees and hear clips of interviews with them.

HORSES AND PONIES

From the Novel

When Ada first sees Butter, she can't believe her luck. She forms an immediate attachment to the pony, and as she rides, she feels empowered.

Horses are widely used with young people who have physical and emotional disabilities. Movement on a horse can be enjoyable. A horse can leap, gallop, and **canter**—movements that are exhilarating for the rider. Also, animals can be comforting. They are not judgmental and do not have prejudices.

Riding sidesaddle, like Ada does, is uncommon today. Ada rides this way because it allows her to control Butter with only one leg, but historically, women rode sidesaddle for modesty's sake. It wasn't considered very ladylike to straddle a horse! Safety skirts were invented in the late 1800s to keep women's skirts from getting caught as they rode, which could be dangerous. Susan kindly makes a pair of **jodhpurs**, or riding pants, for Ada so that she can ride more comfortably.

Eager Equestrians

For beginning riders, the world of horses seems to come with its own foreign language. For example, a pony that is "tacked up" has been saddled and bridled. Today's riders first place a pad on the pony, followed by the saddle. Then, the rider tightens the girth. Next comes the bridle. After putting reins over the pony's head, the rider puts the bit in its mouth and the crown piece around its ears. Finally, the noseband and throatlatch are buckled shut.

WORLD WAR II AND BRITAIN

From the Novel

When the novel opens, the war is just beginning. Ada and Jamie know little about how it will affect their lives. In the months that follow, the danger becomes much more real.

The seeds of World War II were planted when Germany's chancellor, Adolf Hitler, and his Nazi Party came to power in 1933. As the decade wore on, Germany took over Austria and parts of Czechoslovakia. Italy and Japan were also gaining power. Hitler and Benito Mussolini, the Italian **dictator**, joined forces and eventually, along with Japan, formed the Axis powers. In response, France and Britain teamed up against these aggressive, dictator-run countries.

Adolf Hitler

On September 3, 1939, World War II officially began.
Germany seized an area in Poland. France and Britain had promised
to aid Poland, Romania, and Greece if they were attacked. They kept
their promise, and Europe was at war.

LIFE IN WARTIME

From the Novel

As the war began, the British were just beginning to learn all the ways life would change. **Rationing** was new. Susan assures Jamie and Ada that they won't starve. She promises they'll have enough to eat despite the limited food supply.

During the war, people ate more dried and canned foods and were encouraged to grow their own food in a **Victory Garden**. **Propaganda** posters began to spring up. They were often cheerful reminders to citizens to "Dig for Victory," "Grow Your Own Vegetables," or "Fight Famine by Canning Food at Home."

Fighting at Home

"Make-Do and Mend" was a popular slogan of the time. Instead of buying new clothing or linens, people were encouraged to fix what they had so factories could manufacture materials for soldiers and the war. Even rags were considered useful. Ragmen would come by and collect old clothing and blankets that could be salvaged for the war effort.

There are countless ways to get the news today, but in 1940s Britain, the options were limited. Families could listen to the news on the radio, read the newspaper, or watch newsreels that would play prior to movies at the theater.

TVs were not common, so newsreels were ideal for citizens to get information about the war. Some reels showed actual combat, which brought the reality of war home. Others shared uplifting stories or showed politicians discussing current events.

CHURCHILL
U.S. 5 CENTS

Still Fig
Nazis Fierce
CHECK

DUNKIRK

From the Novel

Ada's role in the evacuation of Dunkirk is to help care for the soldiers who arrive daily. They are exhausted, wounded, and traumatized. It's a life-changing experience for Ada, who glimpses her own bravery and strength as she helps the soldiers.

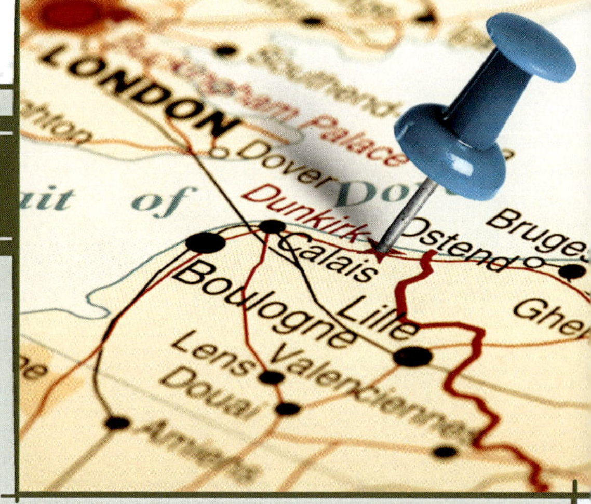

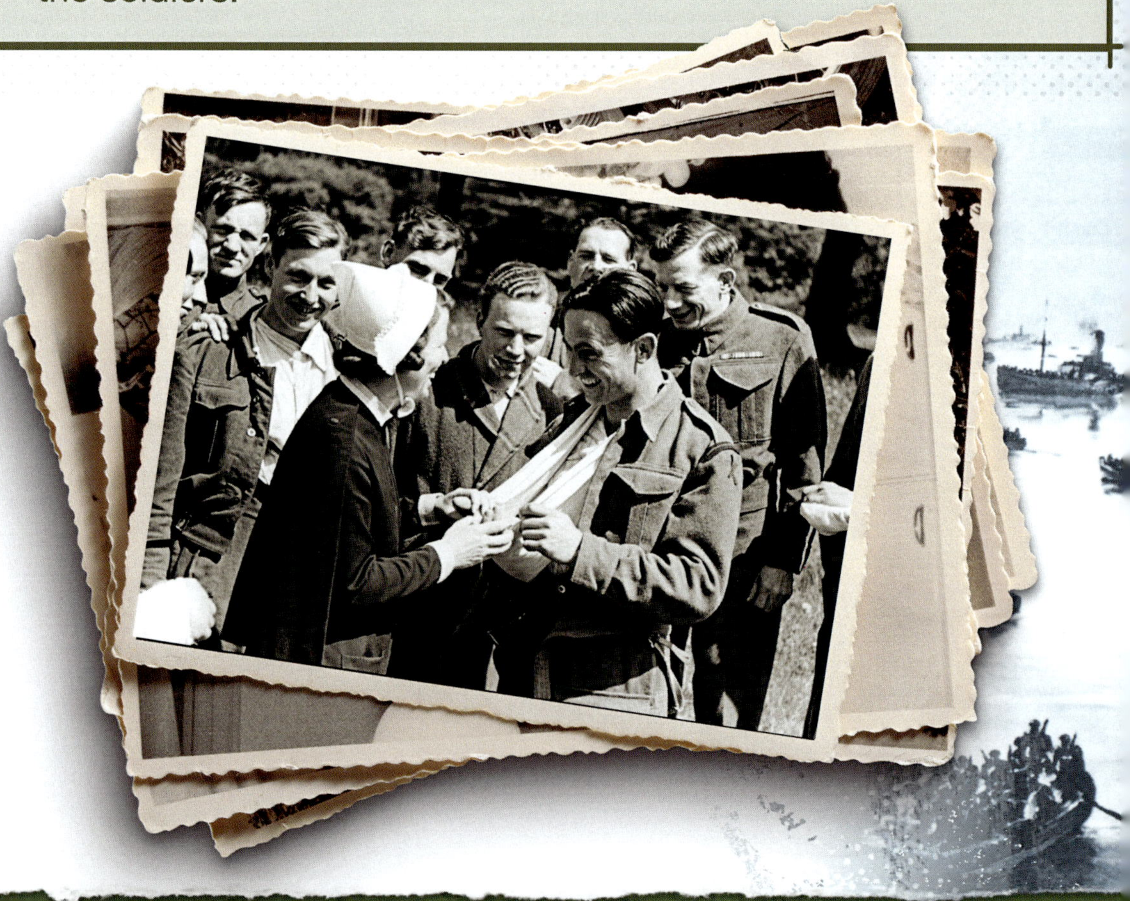

In late May of 1940, the German army had Allied troops trapped at Dunkirk, a French coastal city on the English Channel. At the last moment, Hitler pulled back German troops. The exact reason for this is not known. It gave the Allies a chance to evacuate, but the challenge of how to do it remained.

British Prime Minister Winston Churchill ordered all small boats to head across the English Channel in a rescue mission. No one knew how many soldiers needed rescuing, but estimates were around 45,000. By June 4, nearly 340,000 Allied servicemen were rescued! More than 900 British boats came to their aid, including fishing boats, lifeboats, tugboats, and pleasure boats.

The Dunkirk evacuation served as a great morale booster for Britain. To this day, people use the expression "Dunkirk spirit" to describe the British ability to pull together in hard times.

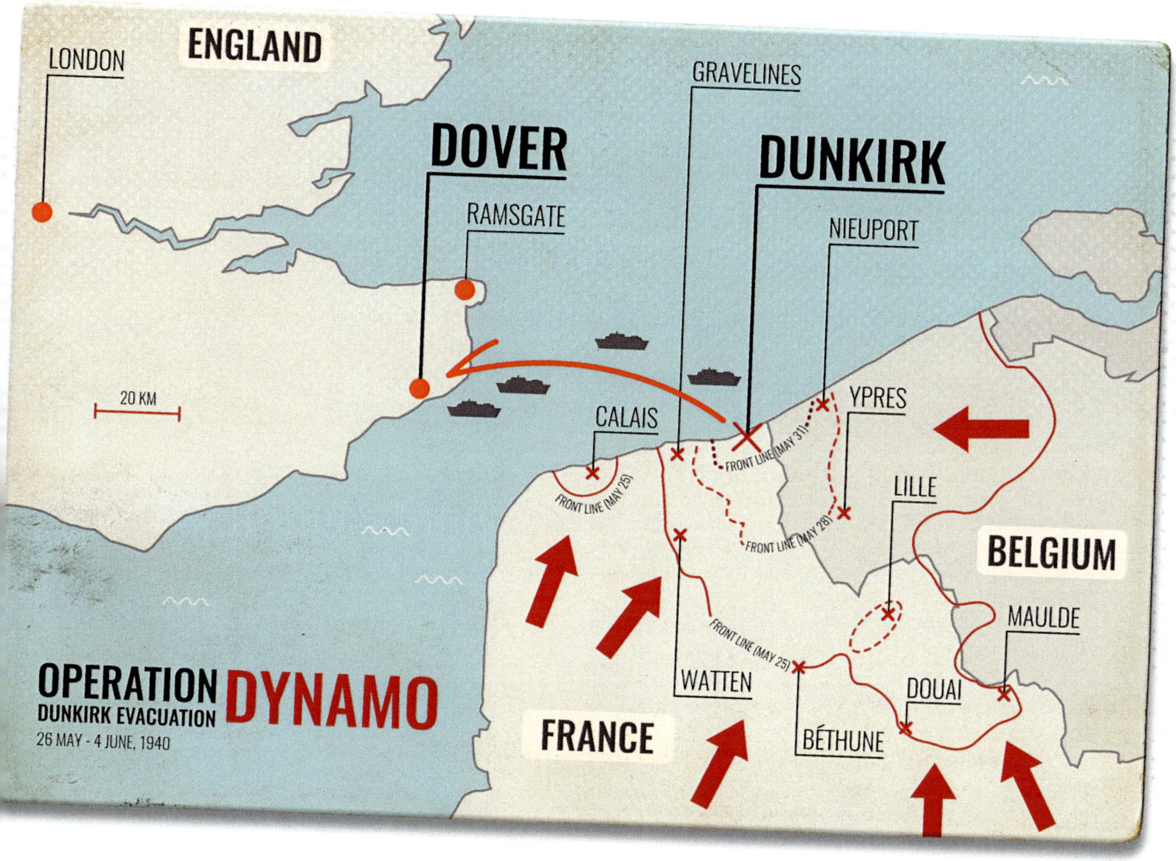

Dunkirk

The evacuation at Dunkirk was a success and saved many lives. Even so, a vast amount of equipment was lost. The Germans sank more than 200 rescue boats, and vehicles, guns, and ammunition had to be left behind. Winston Churchill praised the British but reminded them that "Wars are not won by evacuations."

AIR RAID!

From the Novel

When volunteers build a bomb shelter in Susan's yard, Ada hopes she will never have to use it. It reminds her of the dark cabinet her mother ordered her to crawl inside. Before long, sirens at the airfield go off, and Ada, Jamie, and Susan spend many nights huddled in the underground structure.

The German air force, or **Luftwaffe**, began an intense attack in the summer of 1940. The odds were against the British, but the RAF (Royal Air Force) fought bravely. For every British plane that went down, two Luftwaffe airplanes were destroyed.

On the ground, British citizens did their part. They tried to block any trace of light from homes and businesses that might provide a target for German bombs. They did this by hanging blackout curtains in every window. Volunteers patrolled towns, making sure they were completely blacked out.

The British people listened for sirens that warned of an impending air raid. Then, they rushed into the air raid shelters. Some homes, like Susan's, had private shelters. In big towns and cities, people crowded together in huge communal shelters or underground subway stations and tunnels.

Taking Cover!

Susan's yard had an Anderson shelter. This type of backyard shelter, named for British Home Secretary Sir John Anderson, fit six people. It was made of steel or iron panels bent in a semicircle and covered with dirt. Millions of them were built during the war.

From the Novel

Similarities between the Anderson shelter and the cabinet where Ada's mother punished her make her feel confused and scared. The bunker reminds Ada of an unsafe time in her life. Emotions such as worry, fear, and anxiety overwhelm her, and she needs Susan's help.

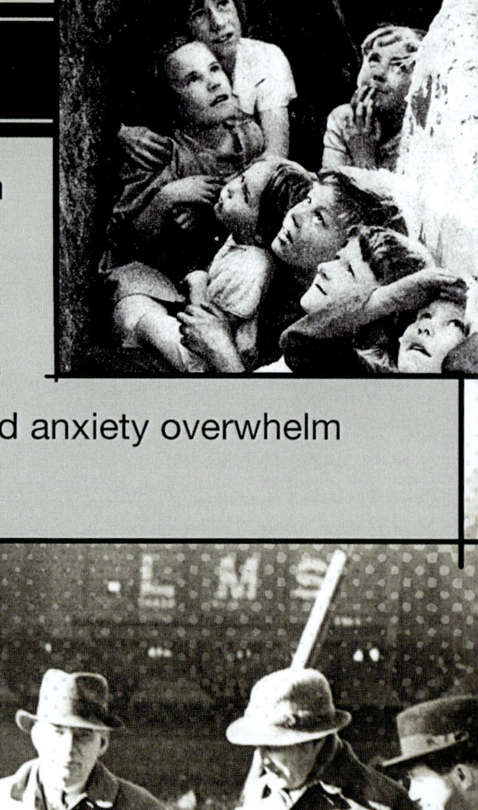

Anderson shelter

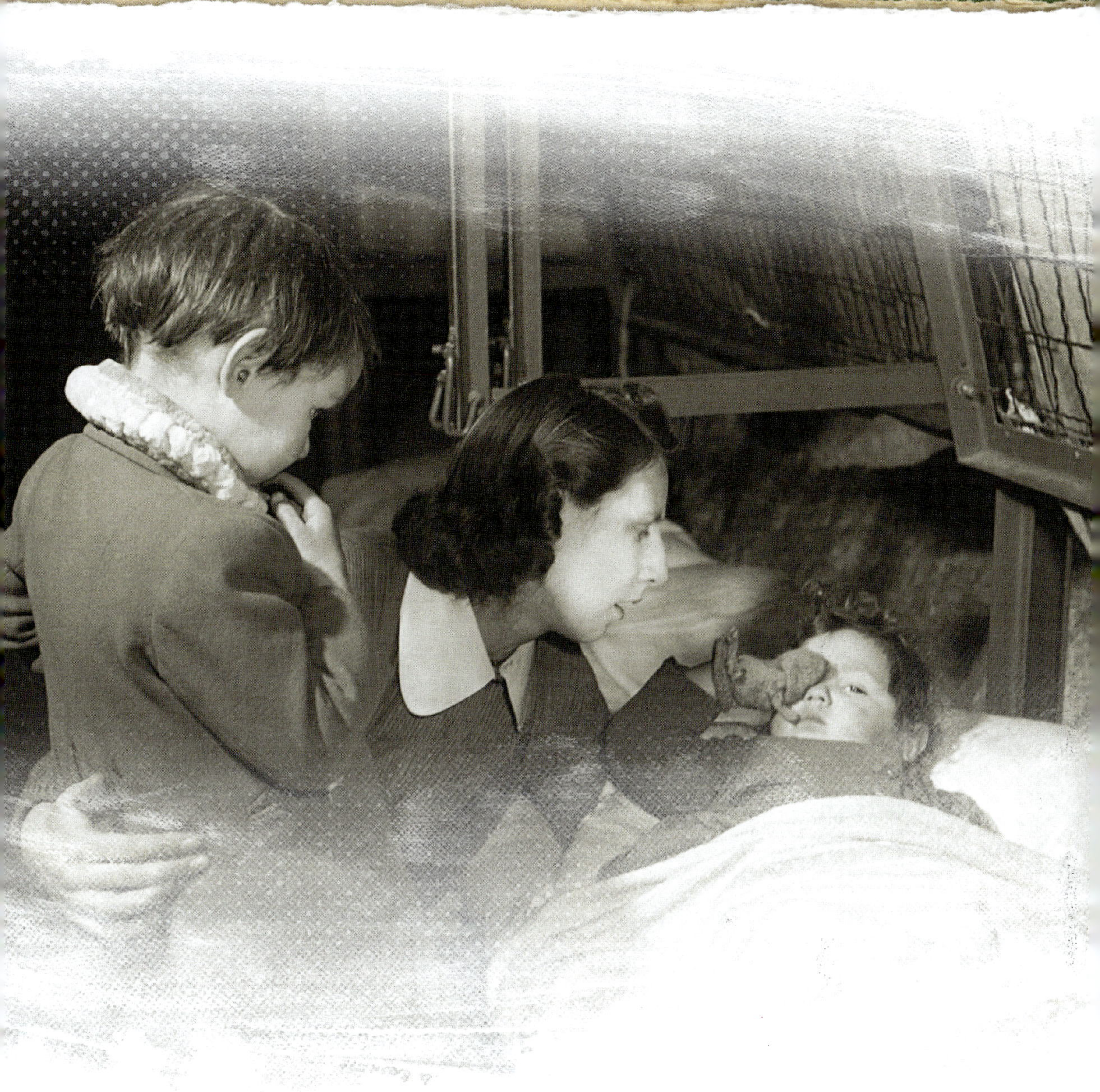

Everyone experiences some or all of those feelings, but some people experience them more frequently or strongly than others. These feelings can grow and become so overwhelming that they negatively affect a person's life, like they sometimes do for Ada.

If you find yourself feeling like Ada does, it's important to reach out to an adult you trust for help.

SPIES

From the Novel

Although Ada is not sure if she exactly believes in spies, she knows that she is supposed to be on the lookout for them. The idea of spies is both exciting and frightening to her.

All kinds of gadgets were used to assist spies in their work. A lot of creativity went into their design! For example, a playing card could hide part of a map beneath its image. A tiny camera could fit inside a matchbox. The heel of a boot could conceal a hiding place for a message. Even a suitcase radio could transmit messages using Morse code. Ada might have seen something like this being buried on the beach.

The Enigma machine was an encryption device used by Nazi Germany to protect military communication.

In Plain Sight

The best sort of spies were people you'd never suspect. You may have read the books Charlie and Chocolate Factory *or* Fantastic Mr. Fox. *The author, Roald Dahl, was a British spy who worked in the U.S., gathering intelligence and trying to get America to join the war against Germany.*

WOMEN AND WAR

From the Novel

Lady Thornton has to convince Susan to join the WVS (Women's Volunteer Service). Susan refers to the women of the group as "wretched do-gooders." They aren't, of course, but Susan is worried that they won't accept her.

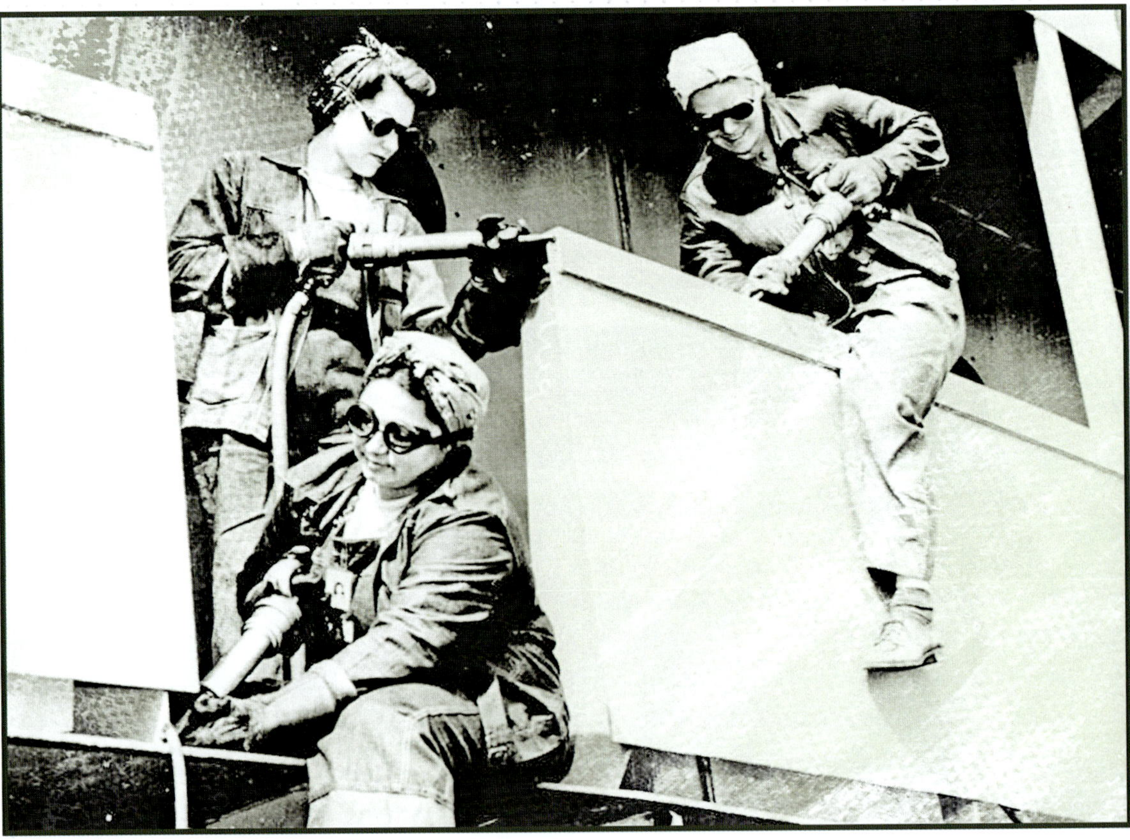

Women were the unsung heroes of World War II, though most would never think of themselves that way. Women took care of their families while the men were away fighting. They ran the household, parented their children, dealt with rationing, recycled as much as possible, and grew a garden if they could. But this was just the start of their work.

Wartime Groceries

Trying to make the most of a family's food rations was a job that fell mostly to women. Here's an example of weekly rations in Britain for one adult:

- *113g bacon and ham (about 4 ounces)*
- *227g other meat (about 8 ounces)*
- *57g butter (about 2 ounces)*
- *57g cheese (about 2 ounces)*
- *113g margarine (about 4 ounces)*
- *113g cooking fat (about 4 ounces)*
- *3 pints of milk (6 cups)*
- *227g sugar (about 8 ounces)*
- *57g tea (about 2 ounces)*
- *1 fresh egg*

Before the war, most women didn't have jobs outside the home. The war changed everything. Women were needed in factories, as bus and fire engine drivers, and as mechanics and engineers. Women even joined the armed forces, though not in combat roles. Instead, they worked as nurses, flew unarmed planes, and even worked as spies for the Special Operations Executive.

Women were suddenly allowed to show their strengths and capabilities. They finally had a chance to shine at jobs that were traditionally for men only.

There is much to learn about WWII and Britain in the 1940s. Keep reading and researching on your own to make more connections between historical facts and *The War That Saved My Life*.

DISCUSSION QUESTIONS

1. Why do you think Bradley based her fictional town on Kent?

2. Explain the meaning and origin of the expression "Dunkirk spirit."

3. Compare how people got their news in 1940s Britain with the way we get our news today. Do you think one method is better than the other?

4. Why were poor children more likely to become ill during the war?

5. How do you think Ada's life might have been different if she had not been sent to the country during the war?

6. How do you think women felt about their expanded roles during the war? Why?

WRITING PROMPTS AND PROJECTS

1. It is very difficult for parents and children to be separated from one another. Find some first-person accounts of evacuees in World War II, either online or at the library. What effects did the memory of this separation have on them throughout their lives?

2. Look up slogans that were popular in England during World War II. Make your own propaganda poster that illustrates the slogan you chose.

3. You've learned about the roles of British women during the war. Do some reading about American women during World War II. How were their roles different from and similar to British women?

4. Search for more information about Victory Gardens. Draw a sketch of a Victory Garden that you would have planted. Explain what you would include and why.

5. Who plans the meals and makes the grocery lists in your family? Would you be able to make do on typical World War II rations?

   - Ask your parent or guardian if you can have a completed grocery list or borrow a current list and copy down the items.

   - Use the sample ration list on page 41 as a guide and multiply each item by the number of people in your family. (For example, if there are four people in your family, you would be able to purchase 8 ounces of butter [2 ounces x 4] a week.)

   - Compare the grocery list with the rations list.

   - Would your family have enough rations to buy a typical week's worth of groceries? If not, what kinds of substitutions could you make?

GLOSSARY

air raids (air reyds): attacks by air

apprenticeship (uh-PREN-tis-ship): a position in which a person learns a trade by working with someone in the field

canter (KAN-ter): to move at a slow, smooth gallop

chilblains (CHIL-bleyns): a condition in which the hands and feet become inflamed due to exposure to the cold

dictator (DIK-tey-ter): a person who has absolute, or complete, control

evacuate (ih-VAK-yoo-eyt): to leave a place, often for reasons of safety

jodhpurs (JOD-pers): riding pants that are full around the hips and fitted at the knees to the ankles

Luftwaffe (LOOFT-vahf-uh): the German air force

malnutrition (mal-nyoo-TRISH-uhn): a state of unwellness due to a lack of healthful, nutritious foods

propaganda (prop-uh-GAN-duh): the public spreading of ideas to help a particular cause

rationing (RASH-uhn-ing): a system in which an item, such as food or clothing, is limited so that everyone can receive a share

Victory Garden (VIK-tuh-ree GAHR-dn): a vegetable garden that helps increase food production during a war

BIBLIOGRAPHY

Adams, Simon. Eyewitness World War II. New York: DK Publishing, Inc., 2007.

Bradley, Kimberly Brubaker. *The War That Saved My Life.* New York: Puffin Books, 2015.

BBC. "Kent During WW2." Last modified March 18, 2008.
http://www.bbc.co.uk/kent/content/articles/2006/06/27/history_kent_during_ww2_feature.shtml.

Gov.uk. "The Women of the Second World War." April 16, 2015.
https://www.gov.uk/government/news/the-women-of-the-second-world-war.

Grochowski, Sarah. "Four Questions for Kimberly Brubaker Bradley," Publishers Weekly, October 3, 2017,
https://www.publishersweekly.com/pw/by-topic/childrens/childrens-authors/article/74957-four-questions-
with-kimberly-brubaker-bradley.html.

Imperial War Museums. "Growing Up in the Second World War." Accessed May 16, 2020.
https://www.iwm.org.uk/history/growing-up-in-the-second-world-war.

Mawson, Gillian. *Britain's Wartime Evacuees: The People, Places and Stories of the Evacuations Told by the People Who Were There.* United Kingdom: Frontline Books, 2016.

Richter, Judy. *Riding for Kids*. North Adams: Storey Publishing, 2003.

INDEX TERMS

ABOUT THE AUTHOR

Lisa Kurkov lives in Charlotte, North Carolina, where she and her husband homeschool their two children. When her head isn't buried in a book, Lisa enjoys baking, crafting, photography, birding, and adventuring with her family.

PHOTO CREDITS: page 1: lSerg/Getty Images; page 4: AiWire/Newscom; page 5: talexkotlov/Getty Images; page 5: spxChrome/Getty Images; page 5: simpson33/Getty Images; page 6: Caron Badkin/Shutter Stock; page 7: abadonian/Getty Images; page 7: nazlisart/Getty Images; page 8: Drimafilm/Getty Images; page 8: Mirrorpix/Newscom; page 9: traveler1116/Getty Images; page 9: akg-images/Newscom; page 9: subjug/Getty Images; page 9: filmstudio/Getty Images; page 10: sergeyryzhov/Getty Images; page 11: Petardj/Getty Images; page 11: AGLPhotoproductions/Getty Images; page 12: U.S. Information Agency; page 13: The Print Collector Heritage Images/Newscom; page 13: Tolga TEZCAN/Getty Images; page 14: Staff/Mirrorpix/Newscom; page 14: Daily Mirror Mirrorpix/Newscom; page 15: Mirrorpix/Newscom; page 15: blueclue/Newscom; page 15: Trifonov_Evgeniy/Getty Images; page 16: T Lea Mirrorpix/Newscom; page 17: tMirrorpix/Newscom; page 17: subjug/Getty Images; page 17: Gearstd/Getty Images; page 18: cynoclub/Getty Images; page 19: ClarkandCompany/Getty Images; page 20: Nadezhda_Nesterova/Getty Images; page 21: duncan1890/Getty Images; page 21: Allusioni/Getty Images; page 22: NNehring/Getty Images; page 23: The Print Collector Heritage Images/Newscom; page 24: World History Archive/Newscom; page 24: Everett Collection/Newscom; page 25: Pictures From History/Newscom; page 25: Staff/Mirrorpix/Newscom; page 26: dja65/Getty Images; page 26: Elzbieta Sekowska/ShutterStock; page 26: whitemay/Getty Images; page 27: sinopics/Getty Images; page 27: nopow/Getty Images; page 27: Everett Collection/Newscom; page 28: malerapaso/Getty Images; page 28: Mirrorpix/Getty Images; page 28: Underwood Archives/UIG Universal Images Group/Newscom; page 28: malerapaso/Getty Images; page 30: The Print Collector Heritage Images/Getty Images; page 31: ploy2907/Getty Images; page 31: bluevlue/Getty Images; page 31: akg-images/Newscom; page 32: greeneyedlens/Getty Images; page 32: kevinruss/Getty Images; page 33: jtyler/Getty Images; page 33: icholakov/Getty Images; page 34: U.S. Information Agency; page 35: The Print Collector Heritage Images/Newscom; page 35: Peter Llewellyn/Getty Images; page 36: World History Archive/Newscom; page 36: Marsh/Mirrorpix/Newscom; page 37: JT Vintage/Zuma Press/Newscom; page 38: Everett Collection/Getty Images; page 38: tMirrorpix/Newscom; page 39: Dennis Brack/Black Star/Newscom; page 39: akg-images/Newscom; page 40: Photri/Polaris/Newscom; page 40: AiWire/Newscom; page 41: AiWire/Newscom; page 41: chrisdorney/Getty Images; page 41: whitemay/Getty Images; page 42: Cole/Mirrorpix/Newscom; page 43: Everette Collection/Newscom; page 44: Photos.com/Getty Images; cover: Zeferli/ Getty Images; cover: eugenesergeev/Getty Images; cover: jtyler/Getty Images; cover: whitemay/Getty Images; cover: duncan1890/Getty Images; cover: GBlakeley/Getty Images; page n/a: enjoynz/ Getty Images; page n/a: -slav-/Getty Images

Library of Congress PCN Data

Nonfiction Companion to Kimberly Brubaker Bradley's The War That Saved My Life / Lisa Kurkov

(Nonfiction Companions)

ISBN 978-1-73164-338-4 (hard cover)

ISBN 978-1-73164-302-5 (soft cover)

ISBN 978-1-73164-402-2 (e-Pub)

ISBN 978-1-73164-370-4 (e-Book)

Library of Congress Control Number: 2020945093

Rourke Educational Media

Printed in the United States of America

04-3472111948

Edited by: Madison Capitano

Cover and interior design by: Joshua Janes